Deutsch? Kein Problem!

Strategies and Resources for Special Needs

Susanne Borgwart
Bitterne Park School, Southampton

Sue Brown
Stoke Damerel Community College, Plymouth

Hampshire County Council

JOHN MURRAY

Also in this series:
Deutsch? Kein Problem!
cassette/song booklet pack by Susanne Borgwart and Elissa
Collins. ISBN 0 7195 7281 9
**Le Français, c'est facile! Strategies and Resources for
Special Needs** by Sue Brown and Sue Dean.
ISBN 0 7195 7100 6
Le Français, c'est facile! Songs for Special Needs
cassette/song booklet pack by Elissa Collins. ISBN 0 7195 7110 3

Acknowledgements

Many thanks to Sue Dean for her work on updating
the Programme of Study Part 1 references and for
her invaluable advice throughout.

© Susanne Borgwart, Sue Brown, Hampshire County Council 1996
First published in 1996 by John Murray (Publishers) Ltd
50 Albemarle Street, London W1X 4BD

A CIP record for this book is available from the British Library.

Cover design by John Townson/Creation

Layouts by Mick McCarthy

Illustrations by David Anstey and Chris Mutter

Typeset by Wearset, Boldon, Tyne and Wear

Printed in Great Britain by St Edmundsbury Press,
Bury St Edmunds.

ISBN 0 7195 7280 0

Contents

General introduction

With the National Curriculum statement that, 'In principle all pupils with special educational needs should have the opportunity to experience a modern foreign language', a languages for all policy became a reality, and not before time. However, this positive move created the need for foreign languages to be made accessible for the whole ability range, and it was from this need that the *Deutsch? Kein Problem!* resource was developed.

Who is it for?

The pupils involved

More than 30% of pupils experience learning difficulties at school; they require a resource to meet their particular needs. This resource aims to interest, motivate and successfully teach them.

The some 2% of pupils with Special Needs statements will be mainly in Special Schools, although increasingly they are integrated into mainstream schools; some will already be in mainstream, with close links with its Special Needs Department. The majority of the target pupils will, however, be in mainstream without the extra support that a statement brings.

Amongst all of these pupils there will be many with very specific, individual needs in German, which a variety of teaching and support staff will need to meet.

The teaching staff involved

In Special Schools the policy of entitlement in languages has given rise to a situation in which many teachers whose expertise is in Special Needs teaching rather than language teaching are faced with providing, in a very limited time, the best they can by way of an introduction to German and the German way of life. This is often being done with great enthusiasm and energy, but also on a shoe-string budget, and without enough time for planning or for the preparation of resources. This resource aims to provide an affordable, accessible pack of materials which will supply these teachers with most of what they need to plan and to resource their German teaching for Key Stage 3.

In mainstream schools non-linguist staff in Special Needs Departments are often providing support for pupils in years 7, 8 and 9, explaining, simplifying and generally differentiating materials on the spot or, at best, for the next lesson. The pack hopes to provide Special Needs Departments with a flexible, clear resource which staff can tailor to individual needs.

Modern Languages Departments in most mainstream schools may have plenty of resources that staff can dip into to create differentiated material for pupils with various learning difficulties. What they, too often, do not have is the time to do this or to make the activities attractive. Moreover, with the materials available, they may not be able to differentiate sufficiently to cater appropriately for the least able. For these teachers this resource provides a ready source of worksheets and activities which take only minutes to make up, and which can be virtually individually tailored.

The value of using *Deutsch? Kein Problem!*

Linguistic values

- Pupils will experience success through learning and using German, the success in itself being as important as the obvious functional value of being able to operate in a foreign language.
- More generally, they may also experience:
  – training for listening
  – re-learning to read
  – practice in copy-writing and writing from memory
  i.e. general linguistic development which may have been missed in early childhood.
- All of these experiences happen in a friendly, stress-free, supportive environment, which is very conducive to the development of language skills.

Educational values

- The resource aids general learning through developing cross-curricular links and skills.
- It aids and improves memory.
- It enables pupils to communicate more effectively.
- It allows the recycling of concepts not previously understood, without loss of self-esteem.
- It provides a challenge.
- It helps to fulfil the right of every pupil to a broad and balanced curriculum.

Personal and social values

- It encourages pupils to work in co-operation with others, as well as individually.
- It develops self-confidence through success. Steps are small and manageable and can be achieved regularly and often.
- It widens experiences and, therefore, horizons.

- It gives opportunities for learned social behaviour (through simulation, role plays, etc.).
- It encourages tolerance and understanding of other people and other cultures.
- It increases self-esteem through the opportunities for achievement and success.

The components of *Deutsch? Kein Problem!*

The following list is a brief summary of the components of this resource. For details of how the resource should be used, see the **Practical introductions** on pages 8–14.

- **A detailed Scheme of Work** for the nine modules, i.e. a structured framework for planning, including communicative and linguistic objectives, and setting out suggested resources, activities and final assignments. The Scheme of Work also outlines opportunities for assessment and explains how the resource is designed to meet the requirements of the National Curriculum.
- **Pictures** which exactly match the vocabulary included, and which can be easily reduced or enlarged to use with a whole variety of suggested activities (see pages 157–82).
- **Worksheet templates** for a variety of practice, reinforcement and assessment activities (see pages 16–41).
- **Suggestions for games** and the templates for making these, using the pictures supplied (see pages 43–88).
- Other **photocopy masters** for classroom use.
- **Teaching notes** at the end of each of the modules giving details of any content or methodology not previously explained in the introduction to the resources and activities.
- **Explanatory notes** on all of these materials written with non-linguist teachers in mind.

Special features of *Deutsch? Kein Problem!*

Flexibility

- Within the suggested linguistic objectives (vocabulary and phrases) for each module, teachers can choose the most relevant and appropriate elements as well as tailor the amount of content to the group or individual.

- The pictures have a large number of suggested uses but teachers may use them as they wish, with a wide range of sizes available. They may be copied onto OHT or can be used to make concept keyboard overlays. They can also be used to make cards for the Language Master.
- Within the suggested activities teachers may again pick and choose depending on the interest, needs, behaviour and mood of the group, or the time available, or the timing of the lesson in the day or the week.
- Worksheets cover a variety of skills and levels and all but Set 1 lend themselves to a wide variety of uses.
- The games come with suggestions for playing them at various levels and teachers or pupils will inevitably think up new variations of old games.
- Topics and linguistic objectives are regularly revisited, giving pupils either the opportunity to learn again what was not fully understood the first time or to re-use known material in a new situation or context. (See content mapping matrix on page 7.)

Ease of use

- The materials have been produced in such a way that teachers, support staff or classroom assistants should be able quickly and easily to make up worksheets, activities or games, as and when individuals or small groups need them, as well as the general preparation of whole class materials for the basic Scheme of Work.
- Blank templates serve as an outline for production of materials.
- Pictures are produced on an easy sliding scale of reproduction for either enlargement or reduction.
- The instructions for use, in the general introduction to the resources and in teaching notes for each module, are clear and straightforward.
- The Scheme of Work framework provides invaluable guidelines for planning in both the short and the long term.
- Many teachers will appreciate the suggestions for assessment since they cover a range of Attainment Targets and levels for each topic.

The *Deutsch? Kein Problem!* song cassette and booklet

Once pupils have become familiar with the basic vocabulary of a particular topic, this cassette and booklet pack offers opportunities to add an extra dimension to their listening and oral work. The cassette includes (on Side 1) the seventeen 'Framework songs' listed below.

Relationship between the framework songs and their variants and the modules in *Deutsch? Kein Problem!*

Module number in *Deutsch? Kein Problem!*	1	2	3	4	5	6	7	8	9
1 Hallo Mutti!	✓						✓	✓	
Variants		✓				✓	✓	✓	
2 Nummer-Rap	✓		✓						
3 Das Alphabet	✓			✓	✓				
4 Meine Haustiere		✓							
Variants		✓				✓	✓		
5 "Deutsch? Kein Problem!" Rap			✓	✓					
Variants		✓			✓	✓	✓	✓	✓
6 Schul-Blues		✓	✓						
Variants					✓	✓		✓	✓
7 Die Wochentage			✓				✓	✓	✓
8 Zu Hause				✓		✓	✓		
Variants		✓				✓	✓		
9 Einkaufen					✓		✓		✓
10 Die Farben		✓		✓	✓				✓
11 Imbiß Kalypso				✓	✓				
Variants					✓	✓			
12 Wir gehen, wir fahren				✓	✓		✓		
13 Der Markt					✓				
Variants								✓	
14 Die Hobbys					✓	✓		✓	✓
15 Mahlzeit Kalypso					✓	✓			
16 Der Kopf, der Mund		✓						✓	
17 Kein Geld Blues					✓	✓		✓	✓
18 Hallo Ruth	✓								
19 Ein Vogel		✓							
20 Bertie hat…		✓	✓						
21 Kein Blatt!		✓	✓						

These are written around a limited vocabulary based on the linguistic objectives given for the topics in this resource file. For each song, guidelines are given to enable teachers to vary the vocabulary and the theme of the song, while retaining the familiar basic structure and tune. The tunes without words are supplied on Side 2 of the cassette to allow variations of the vocabulary to be used.

All the songs and activities have been either written or adapted by Elissa Collins and Susanne Borgwart, to provide the structure, rhythm, musical range and pace to suit the needs of pupils with learning difficulties.

The resources box on each topic sheet indicates when use of the cassette is recommended.

IT opportunities

Deutsch? Kein Problem! can also be used in conjunction with various IT packages, such as *Meine Welt*. The resources box on some topic sheets indicates when suitable opportunities arise to make use of such packages.

Vocabulary/linguistic objectives

- For each topic there is a list of some 20–25 words deemed essential for effectively teaching the topic. These are suggested examples and teachers may wish to add or substitute their own items, but the lists given form the basis of the topic activities.
- Occasionally the list is longer since the topic invites the teacher to tailor the list to the needs of the class/individual.
- Sometimes there are also extra receptive/ productive phrases which can, again, be used at the discretion of the teacher.
- The vocabulary has been selected to aid pupils as much as possible so, when two words exist in English and German in similar forms, the English word is chosen. (This is sometimes a compromise but it is realistic.)
- Words are listed with definite articles, although, with some pupils, use of articles at all may be inappropriate. What is deemed communicative is always left to the discretion of the teacher and will depend on individual pupils' difficulties, etc.

Introducing new language using a visual (flashcard, OHP picture, object, etc.)

1. See and listen.
   See picture and listen to word.
2. See, listen and repeat.
   See picture, listen to word and repeat.

– Start with vowel sound only.
– Start with stressed syllable.
– Back or forward chaining (tag – burtstag – Geburtstag).
– Group and individual repetition.

Hot or cold?
Picture/object is hidden in the classroom. One pupil tries to find it, being guided by the volume with which class keep repeating a word/question (quiet for 'cold', louder for 'warmer'), e.g. 'Wo ist der Bleistift?'.

3. Listen and recognize.
   Listen and point/hold up flashcard/identify picture on OHP/in book/on worksheet.
   (NB Always number pictures on worksheets or on OHP so pupils can respond by giving the number of the picture. Numbers do not need to be from 1 to 10; they could be from 10 to 100 or 20 to 30, etc.)
   Listen and mime (e.g. for verbs).
   Listen and tick the pictures heard.
   Listen and group or sort (teacher to pupil(s) or pupil to pupil).
   – Put series of pictures in order (e.g. by numbering pictures on worksheet).
   – Put pictures on grid (squares have numbers or letters).

4. Recognize and say.
   Either/or questions with pictures.
   – *Ist das eine Katze oder ein Hund? – Ein Hund. Ist das ein Hund oder eine Katze? – Eine Katze.*
   – *Was ist das? – Ein Hund.*
   – *Hast du einen Hund oder eine Katze? – Ich habe eine Katze.*

Watch my lips!
– Teacher or pupil mouths a word without sound for class to identify.

Through the keyhole
– Picture is partly revealed (keyhole cut-out on OHP).

Flash
– Picture is revealed for a fraction of a second only, e.g. by flipping over a card or quick revealing on OHP.
– Four or five pupils are lined up at the front, each holding a flashcard with reverse of picture to the class. At signal from teacher, they all flip their cards over revealing their picture to the class, until a signal from the teacher (e.g. clap hands) tells them to turn it over again. Class are invited to say who does what, etc. This can be set up as a competition with class being divided into two groups.

Guessing games
– Which picture have I got? (teacher or pupil)

Practical introduction to the Scheme of Work

The framework for *Deutsch? Kein Problem!* is based on the structure of HANSOW; this is a KS3 Scheme of Work for modern foreign languages produced over a period of 18 months by the Hampshire advisory service working in co-operation with over 70 MFL teachers in a series of Inset sessions. The original Scheme of Work was published in 1992, having met its objectives of allowing teachers to plan collectively for the National Curriculum, and of contributing to curriculum development.

It soon became clear that this curriculum plan had benefits beyond its intended mainstream audience. Teachers in Special Schools had already begun to plan in their own schools for meeting their pupils' entitlement to a modern foreign languages experience, and to take part in Inset on modern languages methodology. The need for a coherent context for this work led the teacher advisers for MFL to set up a conference with Special School MFL teachers to investigate the adaptation of HANSOW to match the learning needs of pupils, and the time restraints on the curriculum in Special Schools.

The conference was attended by representatives from over 75% of Hampshire's Special Schools with KS3 pupils with moderate learning difficulties (MLD) or emotional and behavioural difficulties (EBD). The resulting development of the HANSOW SPECIAL Scheme of Work has been characterized by co-operation, and a meeting of minds and experiences. The Scheme of Work has been piloted in Special Schools, reviewed and amended. It is, of course, also designed for use in mainstream schools alongside main course material. Indeed, colleagues in many mainstream schools have expressed interest in using the Special Schools' framework; it would be of particular relevance in planning for differentiation within the mainstream framework.

Structure

The structure of the Scheme of Work is modular, that is to say, it is divided into units of work each relating to a particular area of interest for pupils. There are nine modules; each one has several linked topics. There has been an attempt to revise and re-cycle language through the Scheme of Work, but this should not prevent teachers from changing the order of topics or modules, or from substituting their own ideas in order to suit the circumstances in their particular school. It was assumed at the outset that each module would last approximately one term, but indications from teachers are that this will vary from school to school, that flexibility is essential, and even that some of the topics will be more appropriate in KS4.

Assignments

It was clear from the start that teachers want to concentrate on what their pupils can do with the language they have learned; this is why outcomes from pupils are expressed in terms of **communicative objectives**. In keeping with this principle, possible assignments have been suggested for each module. These are intended to provide a purpose for the work in a module, and ideally have in mind the idea of an 'audience'.

National Curriculum Orders

The Scheme of Work has been checked for compatibility with the new orders for MFL and amendments have been made to ensure that it is completely up to date.

Areas of experience

In KS3, pupils must explore areas of experience A, B and C – **Everyday activities**, **Personal and social life**, and **The world around us**. In KS4, pupils following a full course revisit areas A, B and C and also explore areas D and E – **The world of work** and **The international world**. On each module sheet there is an indication of the areas of experience to which the module is most clearly relevant.

Programme of Study (part 1)

The examples given have been amended to match the opportunities for pupils required in **part 1, Learning and Using the Target Language**. It must be stressed that these are examples only.

Attainment targets and level descriptions

There are opportunities for work in all four ATs, though with less emphasis on AT4 (writing) than on the other three targets. The examples given as **Opportunities for Assessment** are compatible with the level descriptions.

Cross-curricular opportunities

The examples provided are to highlight where opportunities exist for teachers to reinforce aspects of their work with pupils across the boundaries of subjects. These are not statutory.

Mapping of linguistic objectives

This cross-referencing of content indicates where revision naturally occurs and also where known material is used in new contexts.

Greetings	1(i)	7(i)					
Naming	1(ii)	2(i)	7(i)				
Classroom objectives	1(iii)	Throughout Module 3					
Classroom target language	1(iv)	Constant reinforcement					
Alphabet	1(v)	Constant reinforcement					
Numbers	1(v)	4(iii)	5(iii)	9(i)			
Family members	2(i)	6(i)	7(i)				
Parts of the body	2(ii)	8(iii)					
Colours	2(ii)	2(iii)	4(v)	5(iv)	9(iii)		
Pets	2(iii)	7(i)					
Likes and dislikes	2(iv)	3(ii)	3(iii)	5(iv)	6(ii)	7(iii)	8(iii)
Days of the week	3(iii)	6(i)	6(iii)	7(iii)	8(i)		
Position	3(iv)	4(iv)	5(ii)	7(ii)			
House (exterior)	4(ii)	7(ii)					
Rooms	4(iii)	6(ii)	7(ii)				
Furniture	4(v)	6(i)	6(ii)				
Transport	5(i)	7(iv)					
Shops	5(ii)	7(iii)	9(ii)				
Food	5(iv)	6(ii)					
Money	5(iii)	9(i)					
Shopping	5(v)	9(ii)					
Activities	6(i)	8(i)	8(ii)				
Places in town	7(iii)	8(i)	8(ii)	9(i)			
Hobbies	8(i)	9(ii)					

Practical introduction to the resources and activities

The explanations given below on how to use the various components are common to all modules or topics, and will not be repeated in the teaching notes for each topic. The teaching notes that are given for each individual topic are brief guidelines and suggestions specific to the use of resources and activities for that particular topic. All of the resources are uniquely flexible and the uses specified are merely suggestions.

The resources comprise the following:
- Sheets of pictures with the German words on the reverse, linked to lists of vocabulary in the modules/topics. These are provided at the correct size for worksheet use and can be enlarged for games, flashcards, etc.
- Blank templates for worksheets (three sets allowing for differentiation and progression). **Note:** samples of the worksheets are made up ready for use as examples.
- Blank masters for activities and games (excluding bingo). **Note:** samples of selected games/activities are made up as examples (see pages 52–57). Individual topic templates for activities such as bingo (see page 76–88).
- Photocopy masters for shops, days of the week, e.g. for wall display.
- The **Resources** box on the topic sheets is divided into two. The items in the lower section are not supplied.

As has been stated, the aim of this teaching pack is that it should be as flexible as possible. So, although activities are suggested for each topic, the pictures and blank templates that are provided allow teachers quickly and easily to produce tailor-made activities to suit individual needs.

How to use the pictures

Each topic has one, sometimes two, sheets of pictures, one for each of the vocabulary items listed in the Linguistic objectives box on the topic sheet. Blank squares mark the end of each subject area. These master sheets show a maximum of 32 pictures. The pictures are intended to be photocopied at a variety of sizes (always on the principle of A4 to A3 or vice versa, as some photocopying equipment offers only this factor of enlargement or reduction). By this process, the pictures can be adapted for a variety of different uses. The table on page 9 shows how this works.

How to use the worksheets

◆ SET 1

Format
- Thick outlines indicate that the picture is to be affixed; edges also prevent shadow when photocopying cut-outs.
- Thin outlines mean that a picture is to be drawn in by the pupil.
- Double lines for writing indicate that writing is to be copied.
- Single lines for writing mean that the teacher or the pupil (depending on the exercise) is to supply the written word.

Note: teachers may find it useful to code these sheets by using different coloured paper for sheets within sets; or they may prefer to code modules/topics by colour, keeping the worksheets within sections the same.

Use
These four sheets are central to the early stages of learning for each topic. Because they are regularly used, pupils become familiar with the format, understand what is required, and feel secure and confident. The sheets should be used at appropriate times in the early stages of a topic, but not all at once.

Variety is important Pupils soon have the confidence to choose which sheets to do, and even go back to ones they feel the need to revise.

Activities and National Curriculum mapping
Sheet 1
- *Kopiere die Wörter und die Bilder*
  Copy the words and the pictures [AT4:1]
The idea of some kind of recognizable image being produced is to enable understanding to be checked without recourse to the written word or translation. It also encourages the correct copying of the word.
Sheet 2
- *Lies die Wörter und male die Bilder*
  Read the words and draw the pictures [AT3:1]
This shows understanding of the written word.
Sheet 3
- *Sieh die Bilder an und schreib die Wörter*
  Look at the pictures and write the words
  – when access is given to the written word [AT4:1]
  – when the word is written from memory [AT4:2]
This indicates the knowledge of the German words for pictures given.

Enlargement/ reduction at each stage		Approximate size of individual picture/mm	Number of pictures/ sheet A4	A3	Uses of pictures
A3 ↑	x141%	251 x 178	1	2	Flashcards
	x141%	178 x 126	2	4	Small flashcards, display
	x141%	126 x 90	4	8	Large games cards, display
	x141%	90 x 64	8	16	Snap cards, etc.
A4	x141%	64 x 45	16	32	
Photocopy master		45 x 32	32	64	Basic worksheets
A4 ↓	x71%	32 x 23	64	128	Wordsearch, survey, etc.
A5	x71%	23 x 16		128	–

Note:
1. All enlargements are 141% i.e. A4 → A3.
2. All reductions are 71% i.e. A4 → A5.
3. A 90° rotation of the pictures occurs on each enlargement, therefore only half the photocopied sheet is reproduced.
   The other half must be photocopied separately.
4. A 90° rotation of the illustrations occurs on each reduction, therefore two A4 sheets can be reproduced together.

Sheet 4
* *Verbinde die Wörter und die Bilder*
  Join up the words and the pictures [AT3:1]
This indicates the ability to read individual words and to understand meanings.

◆ SET 2

Format
* As before thick outlines mean pictures are to be affixed and thin outlines are for pictures to be drawn.
* However, double lines may now be used for writing phrases/sentences.
* The dialogue boxes are for either gluing pictures or for drawing.

Use
These have a more extended use than Set 1 since they enable vocabulary to be linked to produce a phrase or sentence, for example, colour and animals/clothes, number and furniture, likes/dislikes and school subjects/hobbies. They can also be used as the basis for oral activities. Suggestions for the activities (below) will be less prescriptive than for Set 1 since they are open to a variety of uses by teachers. For example, there are several suitable rubrics for Sheet 1, and teachers should choose and insert the one they wish to use for a particular purpose.

Activities and National Curriculum mapping
Sheet 1 (three possible rubrics)
* *Sieh die Bilder an und kopiere die Sätze*
* *Sieh die Bilder an und schreib die Sätze fertig*
* *Sieh die Bilder an und schreib die Sätze*
Pupils can:
* Look at the pictures and copy the sentences [AT4:2]
* Look at the pictures and complete the sentences [AT4:2]. Here the sentence can have missing words which need to be supplied from the clues given in the pictures.
* Look at the pictures and write the sentences [AT4:3]
Note: before reaching the writing phase pupils can be encouraged to say the appropriate phrase/sentence [AT2] and, where the phrase is supplied, to read aloud.

Resources and activities

Sheet 2 (two possible rubrics)
- *Lies die Sätze und male die Bilder*
  Read the sentence and draw the pictures [AT3:2,3]
The pictures must be drawn in the appropriate order in relation to the elements of the sentence, e.g. *ich liebe Hunde* needs heart then dog. The level achieved will depend upon the complexity of the sentence used.
- *Hör zu und male die Bilder*
  Listen to the sentence and draw the pictures [AT1:2]
As a follow-up activity pupils could then fill in the words.

Sheet 3
- *Schreib die Sätze fertig und male die Bilder*
  Complete the pictures and the sentences [AT3:3, AT4:3]
This is a gap-filling activity where one of the pair of pictures and the other part of the phrase/sentence are supplied, and the pupils complete both elements from the clues given.

Sheet 4 (two possible rubrics)
- *Hör zu und schreib die Namen*
  Listen and write in the words [AT1:2]
Pupils should listen to the teacher and then draw pictures or write names to show either **what** is liked/disliked or **who** likes/dislikes something.
- *Male die Bilder*
  Draw in the correct box
Using vocabulary from given topics, pupils can draw in their own likes/dislikes and this is then a basis for a speaking or writing activity [AT2:2,3, AT4:2,3].

Sheet 5a
- *Sieh die Bilder an und mach einen Dialog*
  Look at the pictures and supply the dialogue [AT2:1]
This is a pairwork exercise with each pupil reading a part in the dialogue.

Sheet 5b
- *Lies die Dialoge mit einem Partner und male die Bilder*
  Read the dialogue and draw the pictures [AT3:2]
This is an information-gap exercise, where one picture and the other part of the dialogue are given with the pupil supplying the corresponding speech and picture.

If this is done as a spoken exercise it is [AT2:3]; if it is written before being spoken in pairs it is [AT4:3].
Note: these could be used with directions and places in the town, questions and answers about likes and dislikes, finding out if someone has, or does, something, etc.

◆ SET 3

Format
Thick and thin outlines have the same significance as in Sets 1 and 2. Small boxes beneath pictures are for pupils to either indicate choice (✓ or ✗) or sequence, i.e. number.

Use
These sheets are intended as simple tests at the end of a module or topic to show pupils what they can do and to indicate to the teacher how much has been assimilated. Since some pupils may never be able to complete these exercises from memory, cues must always be available for those who need them. The tick-box sheet can be used for choices or for indicating the recognition of the sequence of items in a list.

Activities and National Curriculum mapping
Sheet 1
- *Sieh die Bilder an und schreib die Wörter*
  Look at the pictures and write the words [AT4:2]
Here the pupil has to recall and correctly write the word.

Sheet 2
- *Lies die Wörter und male die Bilder*
  Read the words and draw the pictures [AT3:1]
The pupil here indicates understanding of the written word.

Sheet 3
- *Hör zu und kreuz das richtige Bild an*
  Listen and tick or cross the right box [AT1:1,2]
Here the pupil chooses one of four items from spoken information, indicating understanding of the spoken word, or shows he or she has recognized the sequence of items in a list, or the order of events, etc.

Game	Participation		AT	Level
Bingo	individual	depending on level of difficulty of game	1	1.2
Pelmanism	pair/group		3	1
Snap	pair		3	1
Dominoes	group		3	1
Noughts & crosses (OHT)	team		2	1
Beetle	group		2	1
Wordsearches	individual	finding words copying them	3	1
Hangman	pair		4	2
Battleships	pair		1	1

National Curriculum mapping

How to use the games

Rationale

Games are a vital part of the learning process: they have an obvious motivating quality because they are fun, but they are also important because they are a way of using the newly-acquired foreign language in a real way; they are important, too, because they encourage pair and group work and so help in the socialization process which is important for pupils with Special Needs. They are often a time when pupils of all abilities are playing (working!) together with no problems of any kind. Games should not be underestimated; so long as they are well-prepared and well set-up, with pupils clear about ground rules, they allow topics to be practised using a range of skills and fulfilling the basic levels of all four attainment targets. They are particularly important because they encourage the use of memorized language which will eventually enable pupils to achieve more than just these basic levels of attainment.

Making the most of the games

The **Extension** activities are suggestions for further exploiting the games. A game should, generally, be just the beginning of a series of activities and not simply an end in itself. For a start, the games take a fair amount of preparation, so it makes good sense to make full use of them. Secondly, once a game has motivated pupils, it is easy to build on reinforcing activities, without loss of interest or concentration.

Winning

• The pupil who wins or completes a game/activity should call out *Gewonnen!* or *Fertig!*
• Prizes are important to pupils where games are concerned. If teachers have the opportunity to go to a German-speaking country, they should collect things like illustrated wrapped sugar-cubes, hotel/restaurant visitors' cards, publicity sheets from tourist offices; also large bags of German sweets (e.g. *Gummibärchen*) are cheap and go a long way! But otherwise coloured stars, amusing inked stamps, stick-on badges, merits, etc. are fine.

Listening and sorting

Pupils have a set of picture cards which they put on to the numbered squares as they hear the words (template 18). For example, *Nummer 1: die Katze.* This can be done with the whole class or in pairs or on the OHP.

Bingo

This is played as an easy way to reinforce new vocabulary. The more restricted the vocabulary, the easier the level. The ready-made bingo cards are in appropriate shapes for the objects to be used for the game, e.g. food in a basket, etc. This helps pupils to focus on the set of vocabulary being used as well as helping them to categorize items.

Bingo is based on the original number game but with specialized blank templates for pupils to **draw** in (not write) items for themselves, as opposed to having ready-printed cards. The importance of this is that pupils are themselves deciding, within a given topic, what to include, e.g. any five animals from the ten learnt. In this way the game is self-differentiating and yet pupils all still have an equal chance of winning.

Once the items have been drawn onto the template, e.g. food in the basket, the teacher calls out random items (twice). Pupils circle those they have and, when all of their items are circled, they have won.

The winner then calls back the items in German so they can be checked before the prize is claimed. It is important that no English is spoken during the game – translation means disqualification!

Extensions

1. e.g. animals in garden, also rooms/furniture, case/clothes, basket/shopping, etc.

- For the game the pupils draw in, say, five animals.
- Continue the game until three people have won.
- Then pupils can be asked to label their animals [AT4:1,2].
- Pupils may be required to exchange information about each other's animals in the garden [AT2:3].
- Pupils could be asked to write a simple sentence listing the animals in their garden [AT4:3].
- Pupils could colour in appropriate animals as you call out animals and colours [AT1:2].

In all of the written activities pupils can naturally differentiate the level because they may choose to work with or without cue words.

2. e.g. furniture and rooms in the house, also school timetable, row of shops and items for sale, etc.

Here the game is extended in the sense that later games become more and more complicated, requiring more and more understanding, memory, etc.

- **level 1** house outline, five unnamed rooms, and pupils simply put a piece of furniture in each of the five rectangles. They circle each piece as heard.
- **level 2** house outline, five named rooms, and pupils put a piece of furniture in each room. Now they need to listen for the correct room for the furniture they have drawn, i.e. if they have put a chair in the kitchen they can only count it if they hear *Der Stuhl ist in der Küche.* This encourages careful listening and is training for listening for specific detail.
- **level 3** as above, but any number of pieces of furniture are required to be drawn in each room, so that listening skills are extended.

Refer back to Extension 1 and you will see that any activity of that kind done with levels 2 or 3 will naturally be of a higher level of writing, reading or speaking.

Snap

This requires one set of picture cards and a matching set of word cards, or a matching set of German and English word cards.

- Pair game matching German words with pictures, or German words with English equivalent.
- To avoid confusion and aid organization make each set of cards a different colour, i.e.
  – picture cards
  – German words
  – English equivalents
- For each game use German words and one of the other two sets.
- To play, each pupil holds one set of cards face down. In turn, players place their top card face up in front of them.
- If two cards match, the first person to recognize this and say *Gewonnen!* or *Schnipp-schnapp!* claims the pair of cards and keeps them on the table.

- The game is over when either all of the cards have been won, or each set of cards has been gone through with no more matching pairs.
- The game is won by the player with the most pairs.

Extensions (These activities can also be used with Pelmanism.)

- Pupils can be required to count in German the number of cards they have.
- They can inform partner/group of what they are holding or five items that they are holding.
- They can copy into books any three pairs they are holding or which are laid out on the table by the winner.

Pelmanism

- This makes use of the same sets of cards as snap, i.e. German words/pictures or German words/ English equivalents.
- Cards are placed face down on the table.
- Players take turns in turning up one card of each colour and if they match they keep the pair.
- If they do not match, the cards are replaced face down, but they remain in the same place.
- The players should gradually memorize where cards are and this will help them to choose two that match and make a pair.
- When all of the cards have gone from the table, the winner is the player holding most pairs.
- **NB** Where alternatives are given the teacher should choose the word/phrase which suits his/her pupils best – it is not intended that they must learn both – and delete the unwanted version on the master copy.

Extensions (as for snap)

Dominoes

This requires a set of cards with a picture and a word on each 'domino' – from the sample game supplied it will be apparent that, when making up the set, pictures and matching words need to be offset by one card, i.e. the word on the last card will match up with the picture on the first card.

- To ensure that the game can work out, follow the template and example carefully.
- Sets of cards need to be photocopied for groups to play. Copy each set onto different colour card, or number the reverse of sets, so that sets do not get mixed up.
- To play the game, the cards are all dealt out to three or four players.
- One player starts by putting a card down. The next player needs to place a card to match and join up with either picture to word or word to picture, and so on, around the table.
- The player who cannot go misses a turn and play moves on to the next player.
- The winner is the one to use up all of the dealt cards first.

- A score can be kept of how many wins are scored by pupils during any one session (of, say, four games) and then a class prize can be awarded.

Beetle

- This game is for up to six players (which can include a banker).
- Sets of pictures are needed (up to six within each set) and a die.
- The six chosen pictures correspond to a collectable group of items, e.g. set of clothes, food for a picnic, etc.
- The sets of cards need to be numbered 1–6 on the reverse, e.g. hats = 1, coats = 2, etc. (See example, pages 53–54.)
- The pupils take it in turns to shake the die and ask for (or announce and take, if there is no banker) the item which matches the number thrown.
- If the number corresponds to an item already held by the player, that go is missed and the die goes on to the next player.
- 'Banker's cards', showing the six items and their die value, will help pupils ask for what they need.
- The game is won when one player has a complete set of pictures.

Extensions

- When the game is over pupils can exchange information about what they are holding and also what they are lacking, thereby using negatives.
- Everyone in the group could be required to copy into their books the complete set of pictures and then label them.

Noughts and crosses

This is a class team game using the OHP or the white/black board. This makes use of pictures only, and is therefore a memory recognition game and does not include reading. The idea is that the noughts and crosses frame starts off with pictures in its numbered squares. A member of a team (either O or X) picks a number and says in German what the picture is. If the answer is correct the picture is replaced by an O or an X as appropriate. The important thing about this game is that the team can be mixed-ability; **any** individual will be more interested in gaining a useful square, i.e. one which either helps towards a line or blocks a line from the other team, than in the pictures themselves, so will **risk** giving an uncertain word, rather than playing safe with a familiar word, since there is a definite aim in the choice. Too often SEN pupils do not take risks.

Extensions

- This can become a reading game. Pupils show understanding by placing the correct picture with the word/caption, and thus gaining their O or X.
- Complications can be added by having complex pictures or phrases, e.g. like/dislike and item, number and object.

Hangman

This is basically a spelling game played in pairs or teams, but again is self-differentiating, as no-one will choose an unknown word. There is always the risk here that a pupil may spell a word incorrectly, but this is a natural problem in life and hopefully one pupil might pick up the mistake, which will make it part of the learning process.

Wordsearch

Initially words should go horizontally and vertically only. The puzzle may be complicated by using diagonals later, but the words should **never** be entered backwards.

For the puzzle, either the German words that are hidden can be given, or the words and pictures, or just the pictures. The latter is the most difficult since the pupil needs to think what the word is first, then find it.

Extensions

- If just the words are given, when the puzzle is completed a picture could be drawn for each to show comprehension.
- A written task could follow the puzzle, with the word being copied under each picture.

In both cases, learning and spelling are being reinforced.

Blank wordsearches can also be given to pupils to make up their own puzzles. This is not only creative (important for the National Curriculum), but it is also a meaningful task, since pupils can then swap puzzles.

Battleships

The basic game uses a grid with numbers across the top and letters down one side. Pupils put given items, e.g. school subjects, into squares and partners find out where each other's vocabulary is hidden by asking 'A4? B3?' etc. Correct guesses are scored as hits, and marked off by each player. The letters and numbers can be varied so that it is not always A1, A2, etc. but A10, A20, A30, etc. or H5, H10, H15 to practise letters which come later in the alphabet or higher numbers.

Extension

- The game is much more communicative, however, if the grids combine two elements of a final sentence e.g. animals across the top, names down the side.
- Players tick their choice of boxes. The players take turns asking, *Hat Sabine einen Hund?* etc. If that square has been ticked the response is *'Ja'* and this is scored as a hit.
- The winner is the first player to locate all the ticks on his/her partner's grid.
- Instead of ticks, five fish can be drawn in the squares (*Fang die Fische!*) The winner is the first person to catch all his/her partner's fish.

Kim's game

This requires a tray, some objects and a cloth to cover the tray. It can be either a simple memory game where pupils, in teams or individually, recall as many of the objects as possible, or, while the tray is covered an object can be removed and then pupils have to name the missing object. This can also be done very effectively with objects or pictures on the OHP.

Extension

- A variation on Kim's game is 'Kim remembers'. Example: OHT of house showing the various rooms and one member of the family in each room. Pupils have 30 seconds to see the picture and to memorize who is in each room (they do not have to remember all of them, of course). If the class can remember all of them correctly, they score a point; otherwise the point goes to the teacher. Like Battleships, this game is extremely flexible and can be used to elicit a wide range of language. 'Kim remembers' can be played to remember (and say or write) who has what, what is where, what colour animals or clothes are, etc.

Guess the rule

This is a good game to get pupils to practise questions or invitations or offering something. No resources are needed.

The teacher makes up a rule according to which some pupils' questions will be answered with 'yes' and other pupils' questions will be answered with 'no', e.g. the teacher has decided to answer with 'yes' to all questions from pupils sitting on the right-hand side of the room, and 'no' to the ones from the left. Pupils are invited to ask questions and to observe the answers until they have worked out what the rule is. For example:

Pupil A (on the left): *Gehen wir ins Kino?* Teacher: *Nein, danke.*

Pupil B (on the right): *Gehen wir ins Schwimmbad?* Teacher: *Oh ja!*

NB Insist on a minimum number of questions from pupils before they have a go at guessing the rule. Make sure the rule is easily observable.

Blank worksheets and examples

Module _____ Topic _____

Kopiere die Wörter und die Bilder: _____

Module _____1_____ **Topic** _____(iii)_____

Kopiere die Wörter und die Bilder:

der Stuhl

das Papier

die Tafel

die Tür

der Bleistift

Module _____ **Topic** _____

<u>Lies die Wörter und male die Bilder:</u>

_____

_____

_____

_____

_____

Lies die Wörter und male die Bilder:

DEUTSCH? KEIN PROBLEM!

Module _____2_____ **Topic** _____(iv)_____

Lies die Wörter und male die Bilder:

ein Vogel

ein Goldfisch

ein Hund

eine Maus

ein Pferd

 © John Murray (Publishers) Ltd **19**

Module _____ **Topic** _____

Sieh die Bilder an und schreib die Wörter:

_____

_____

_____

_____

_____

Module _____2_____ **Topic** _____(iv)_____

<u>Sieh die Bilder an und schreib die Wörter:</u>

_____

_____

_____

_____

_____

Module _____ **Topic** _____

Verbinde die Wörter und die Bilder:
....

DEUTSCH? KEIN PROBLEM!

Module _____3_____ **Topic** _____(i)_____

Verbinde die Wörter und die Bilder:

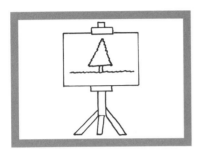

Musik

Mathe

Sport

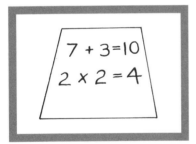

Kunst

Deutsch

Module _____ **Topic** _____

Module _____3_____ **Topic** _____(ii)_____

Sieh die Bilder an und schreib die Sätze fertig :

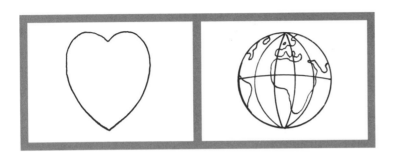
_____

_____ Erdkunde

Ich mag _____

_____ nicht so gern

Ich liebe _____

_____

_____

Informatik _____

Module_____ **Topic**_____

Module _____ 5 _____ **Topic** _____ (iv) _____

Lies die Sätze und male die Bilder:

Ich möchte ein Bier
und eine Cola, bitte.

Ich möchte eine Bratwurst
und ein Brötchen, bitte.

Ich möchte Kartoffelchips
und einen Apfel, bitte.

Ich möchte Pommes frites
und eine Limo, bitte.

Module_____ **Topic**_____

Schreib die Sätze fertig und male die Bilder: _____

Module _____4_____ **Topic** _____(vi)_____

Schreib die Sätze fertig und male die Bilder: _____

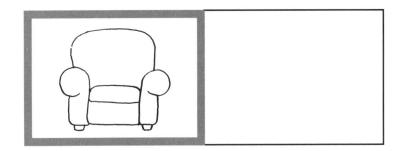

Der _____

ist im Wohnzimmer. _____

Das Bett und der _____

sind im _____

Der _____

ist im Eßzimmer. _____

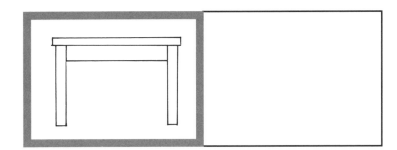

Die Katze ist _____

in der _____

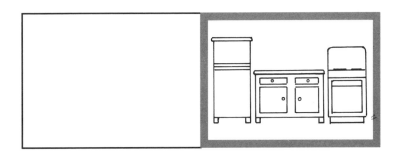

Module_____ **Topic**_____

<table>
<tr><td></td><td></td><td></td><td></td></tr>
<tr><td></td><td></td><td></td><td></td></tr>
</table>

<table>
<tr><td></td><td></td></tr>
<tr><td></td><td></td></tr>
</table>

Module _____5_____ **Topic** _____(iv)_____

Hör zu und schreib die Namen : _____

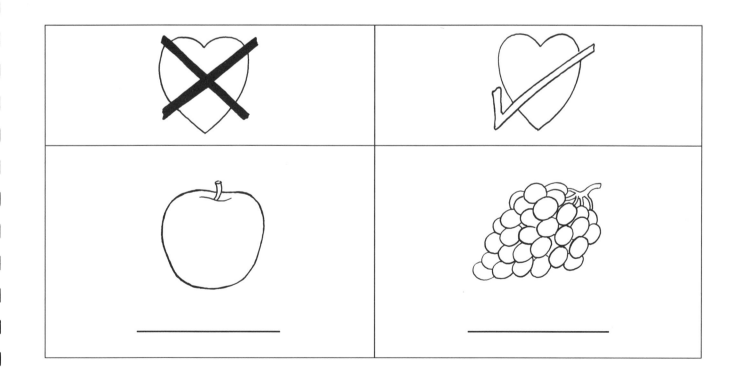

Module_____ **Topic**_____

Sieh die Bilder an und mach einen Dialog:_____

Module _____3_____   **Topic** _____(v)_____

Sieh die Bilder an und mach einen Dialog: _____

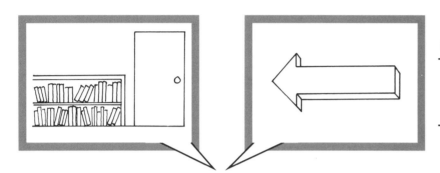

<u>Wo ist die Bücherei?</u>

_____

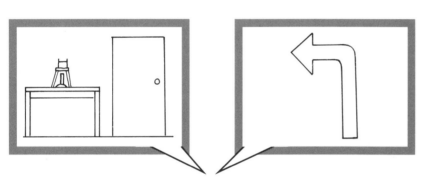

<u>Wo ist der Chemiesaal?</u>

_____

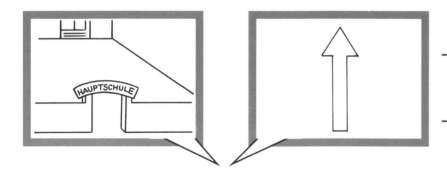

_____ der Schulhof?

_____

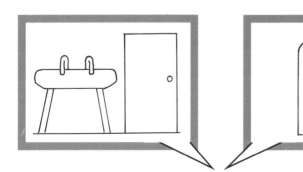

_____ ?

_____

Module_____ **Topic**_____

<u>Lies die Dialoge mit einem Partner und male die Bilder:</u>

Module _____5_____ **Topic** _____(iv)_____

Lies die Dialoge mit einem Partner und male die Bilder:

Was kostet
das Eis?
Zwei Mark

Was kostet
die Bratwurst?
Drei Mark fünfzig

Was kosten
die Äpfel?
Vier Mark das kilo

Was kosten
die Pommes Frites?
Zwei Mark dreißig

Module_____ **Topic**_____

<u>Sieh die Bilder an und schreib die Wörter:</u>

Module _____9_____ **Topic** _____(iii)_____

Sieh die Bilder an und schreib die Wörter:

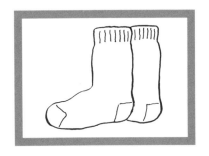

_____

_____

_____

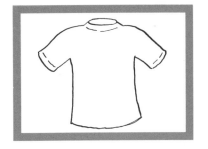

_____

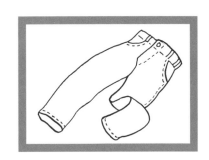

_____

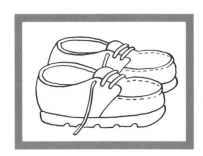

_____

_____

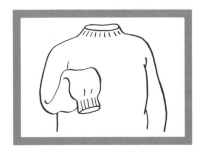

_____

_____

 37

Module_____ **Topic**_____

<u>Lies die Wörter und male die Bilder:</u>_____